Crafty
CRIME-busting

The Knowledge

Crafty CRIME-busting

RACHEL WRIGHT

Illustrated by
Royston Robertson

Hippo

Scholastic Children's Books,
Euston House, 24 Eversholt Street,
London, NW1 1DB, UK
A division of Scholastic Ltd
London ~ New York ~ Toronto ~ Sydney ~ Auckland
Mexico City ~ New Delhi ~ Hong Kong

First published in the Uk by Scholastic Ltd, 2003

10 digit ISBN 0 439 98185 9
13 digit ISBN 978 0439 98185 9

Typeset by Falcon Oast Graphic Art Ltd
Printed in the UK by CPI Bookmarque, Croydon, CR0 4TD

10 9

CONTENTS

INTRODUCTION

AND NOW ... "THAT'S CRIMINAL!" THE TV CRIME PROGRAMME THAT HELPS YOU FEEL SAFER IN THE WORLD

CRIME IS A GROWING PROBLEM. MANY PEOPLE ARE CHOOSING A CAREER OF CRIME IN THE BELIEF THAT IT BEATS WORKING

BUT THE CRIMINAL LIFE IS NO PICNIC. MANY CROOKS WORK LATE, IN PLACES WITHOUT PROPER LIGHTING, HEATING OR TOILET FACILITIES

WHAT'S MORE, CRIMINALS ARE UP AGAINST SKILFUL CRIME-BUSTERS, SUCH AS POLICE DETECTIVES, CRIME SCIENTISTS AND CRIME DOCTORS, WHO HAVE SCORES OF SLEUTHING SURPRISES UP THEIR SLEEVES

HELLO, SECURITY? YES, IT'S HIM AGAIN ...

SO, IF YOU'RE DREAMING OF AN EASY LIFE OF CRIME ... **WAKE UP** AND READ THIS BOOK. YOU'LL SOON DISCOVER HOW SOMETHING AS TINY AS A THREAD OR A SPECK OF BLOOD CAN HELP TO CATCH A VILLAIN

The Knowledge
cr**A**fty
CRIME-bust**ING**

YOU'LL ALSO DISCOVER HOW A FIRED BULLET CAN HELP SNARE A KILLER AND WHY MURDER BY POISON IS A DYING BUSINESS

YOU'LL EVEN BE CALLED IN TO HELP SOLVE SOME BAFFLING CASES YOURSELF.

SO IF YOU WANT TO KNOW WHICH CRIMINAL WAS KIPPERED BY A MIND-READER, OR WHO WAS THE FIRST KILLER TO BE CAUGHT OUT BY A BLOODY THUMBPRINT, GET READING ...

THE FINGERPRINT FILES

No matter how carefully a criminal plans a crime, one thing's for certain. He or she will accidentally leave something behind at the crime scene that wasn't there before, as this true story reveals...

The mark of a murderer
In 1892, two children were found dead in their home in Argentina. They had been hit over the head with a hard object. The children's unmarried mother, Francesca Rojas, immediately accused a ranch worker called Velasquez of the double murder. But Velasquez denied all knowledge of the killings, so the local chief of police decided to try to force a confession.

HERE'S WHAT WE'LL DO: WE'LL LOCK VELASQUEZ IN THE SAME ROOM AS THE DEAD CHILDREN. BY MORNING HE'LL BE SO FREAKED OUT THAT HE'LL CONFESS EVERYTHING!

WANTED

CHIEF

But Velasquez refused to confess.

Meanwhile, gossip about Francesca Rojas had reached police ears. Rumour had it that the unmarried mother had a new boyfriend who had said that he would marry her ... if she were childless. Suddenly Velasquez was no longer the prime suspect. Francesca herself was now in the frame.

Once again the chief of police decided to go for a forced confession. This time he spent the night outside Francesca's home making spooky noises in the hope she'd be so terrified that she'd confess all. But Francesca was not so easily rattled.

Finally the chief of police decided he needed some outside help. Regional headquarters sent an inspector who, unlike the local chief of police, examined Francesca's home thoroughly. Inside, he found the print of a bloodstained human thumb on a door. Wasting no time, the inspector cut out the bloodstained section of the door and took it to the police station. There, he asked Francesca to roll her right thumb on to an inky pad, then on to a piece of paper.

The pattern of swirling lines made by Francesca's inky thumb matched the mark on the door exactly. There could be no doubt that the bloody print had been made by Francesca.

The inspector had proved that she was at the scene of the crime when the crime was committed.

At last, Francesca's steely nerve snapped. She admitted that she had killed her children because they were ruining her chances of marrying her new boyfriend. After hitting them both over the head with a stone, she had chucked the stone into a well and washed her hands ... but not before touching the door.

The case cracked, Francesca Rojas has gone down in history as the first murderer to be caught by a crime scene thumbprint.

Print puzzler

As grisly Francesca found to her cost, fingerprints are a great means of identifying someone because nobody has exactly the same fingerprints as anyone else. But that's not all. Fingerprints are a reliable way of identifying people for other reasons, too. See if you can put your finger on those reasons by answering this quick quiz.

1. The patterns on human fingertips usually remain the same from birth to death. True or false?

2. The only way to erase fingertip patterns is to burn them with acid or rub them with sandpaper. True or false?

3. Fingertip patterns are one of the last bits of a body to rot away after death. True or false?

Answers:

1. True. The patterns on your fingertips were formed by pressure on your hands whilst you were growing inside your mum's tum.

2. False. When the skin grows back, so do the patterns. Having an operation to remove your fingerprints is no guarantee of success, either. In 1941 a convicted robber decided to get rid of his fingerprints by having an operation that replaced the skin on his fingertips with skin from his sides. The op was a great success, and the robber soon robbed again ... only to be promptly arrested. The police had been able to identify him by prints made by the remaining parts of his fingers.

YOU'RE ALL FINGERS AND THUMBS WHEN IT COMES TO ROBBERY

3. True. Fingerprints can be used to identify a corpse months, or even years, after death. In 1933 the skin of a human hand was found near Wagga Wagga in Australia. It looked just like a glove made from human skin. By slipping on the "glove" and fingerprinting it, just as Francesca Rojas's thumb was fingerprinted, crime-busters were able to find out to whom the lifeless hand had belonged ... and who had chopped it off.

Crime-cracking fact
A burglar in Britain thought he was being exceedingly cunning when he took off his socks and wore them as gloves so as not to leave fingerprints. But police soon caught up with him. They identified him by his footprints. As with fingerprints, no two people have the exact same footprints. Nor do they have identical palm-prints or ear prints, either.

DIY fingerprinting

Fingerprint patterns are generally split into three main groups – loops, arches and whorls. Want to discover which group your right thumbprint belongs to? Roll your thumb, from one side of the nail to the other, on a stamp pad, and then on to some plain paper, and compare your print with the patterns below.

LOOPS

PLAIN LOOP

CONVERGING
LOOP

NUTANT
LOOP

ARCHES

PLAIN ARCH

TENTED ARCH

WHORLS

SPIRAL WHORL

TWINNED LOOP

LATERAL POCKET

COMPOSITE

ACCIDENTAL

Finding fingerprints

Fingermarks made by bloody, inky or dirty fingers are easy to see. But fingermarks made up of just oily sweat are hard, or impossible to spot. See for yourself. Wipe a clean, dry drinking-glass inside and out with a tea towel. Then grasp it firmly with one hand, and put it down. It still looks pretty clean, right? Now pick it up at its base and hold it up to an electric light. (It helps if you switch on the light first.) You should just be able to see the fingermarks you left behind when you grasped the glass.

Fingermarks left at crime scenes are often much harder to spot than those you left on that drinking-glass. To those in the know, these invisible fingermarks are called latents, or latent prints. (Fingerprints are sometimes nicknamed dabs, too.) In a sec you'll get a chance to examine a crime scene and to work out where some case-cracking latent prints are likely to be lurking, but first ... here's a report from *Crafty Crime-busting*'s very own crime-cracker, Casey Cracked.

The Files of Casey Cracked

Case: The Drunk Skunk burglary
Report number: 1

Now, drinking alcohol ain't my cup of tea. I'm more of a soft drinks kinda girl. But a job's a job. So when I got a call saying that The Drunk Skunk bar had had a break-in, I was on the case. The bar's owner looked as cheerful as a dying duck. Seems last night he had locked up, swept up and gone upstairs to bed as usual. But when he had come down this morning, the bar's cash till (and cash) were missing.

A woman across the street says she clearly saw two men leaving the bar at midnight, carrying something heavy. But you can't always trust an eyewitness. A victim once told me she'd been attacked by a giant lemon. Turned out she'd been attacked by a large lime. No, I needed more than an eyewitness account. So I poured myself a rum and coke, without the rum, and figured out at least six spots where the burglars' fingerprints might be found.

Where do you think fingermarks made by the burglars might be found? Think carefully about how the burglars got into, and out of, the bar, and how they removed the cash till.

Clue: things that hold fingerprints include paper, painted surfaces, unpainted wooden surfaces, live plants, glass and most metals. (The insides of rubber gloves also hold fingerprints, but unless the burglars did a spot of washing up before they left the bar, you needn't bother about that now.) Things that don't hold fingerprints include most rocks and stones, and bricks.

Answers:

1. The window latch. Most of the shattered glass has fallen into the bar. This suggests that someone broke the glass from outside, then reached in and opened the window.

2. The window frame and sill. The burglars may have held on to the frame whilst climbing through the window.

3. The upturned stool on the counter nearest to the missing cash till. One of the burglars may have pushed this stool further up the counter, to make it easier to slide the cash till off the counter.

4. The stool standing on the floor. One of the burglars may have taken this stool off the counter, to make it easier to remove the till.

5. The light switch. It was dark when the crime was committed, so the burglars may have turned on the lights to help them find their way about.

6. The key and inside handle of the front door. The burglars probably left by this door.

Dab dusting

Figuring out where invisible fingermarks are likely to be lurking is one thing. But making these hidden marks visible to the naked eye, so that they can be collected or photographed, is another kettle of clues entirely. There are a number of methods available for making latent prints visible. The method chosen depends largely on the kind of surface the fingermark is sitting on.

Crime-busting for Beginners

Dusting for dabs
By Phil "Fingers" O'Farrell

Method 1.
To lift latent prints from smooth, nonporous (not absorbent) surfaces such as glass, painted window frames and plastic light switches:

1. Lightly dust some fingerprint powder on to the surface using a fluffy brush. The powder will stick to the lines of oily sweat and make the latent print visible.

2. Press some clear sticky-backed tape down on to the print, lift off the tape, and press it down on a piece of card.

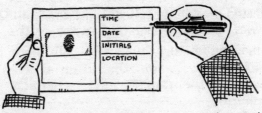

3. Write the time, date and your initials on the card, plus a brief description of where you found the fingerprint.

Method 2.
Rough, nonporous surfaces, such as the grained plastic surfaces inside cars, are best treated by fuming. That's because there's a danger that prints on these surfaces could be brushed away. To lift dabs from the inside of a car:

1. Heat up a substance called cyanoacrylate inside the car, and seal up the car. As the cyanoacrylate heats up, it will create fumes, which will react with any latent prints, turning the prints white and fixing them in place.

2. Once the latents are fixed, you can dust them in the usual way.

Method 3.
There's no point in dusting a stolen cheque for prints, because the oily sweat of the thief's fingerprints will have sunk into the paper. Instead:
1. Spray the paper with a chemical called ninhydrin.
2. Steam iron the paper and wait for the prints to appear.

Method 4.
When investigating a serious crime, such as murder, it's vital not to miss prints in unlikely places. It's also vital not to waste a lot of time dusting for prints in likely spots. Instead:
1. Blackout the room in which the murder took place.
2. Get yourself a portable laser unit, put on a pair of special goggles to protect your eyes, and shine a beam of laser light over every part of the room. This will make the chemicals in any fingerprints fluoresce (glow like a luminous watch-face glows in the dark).

3. Photograph the prints under laser light.

Crime-cracking fact
In the USA, there is a national crime-busting organization called the Federal Bureau of Investigation, or FBI for short. The FBI first used lasers for fingermark-finding in 1980.

Matching fingerprints

Often, many of the fingerprints found at a crime scene can be easily identified because people who live or work at the crime scene left them. Those prints that can't be identified may belong to the criminal. If the police have a suspect (someone they think may have committed the crime), they can compare the suspect's prints with the unidentified crime scene prints. If the prints match up, it proves the suspect was at the crime scene, even if she or he says otherwise (and chances are, she or he *will* say otherwise).

But what happens when police don't have a suspect, or even the shadow of a suspect?

The answer is simple. They compare the unidentified crime scene prints with the computer-recorded fingerprints of people who have been arrested. You see, whenever someone is arrested, a record is taken of his or her fingerprints. In the past fingerprints were recorded in much the same way you recorded your thumbprint on page 13. Now fingerprints are often recorded electronically. First, the fingertips are pressed on to a glass-topped computer unit (livescan unit). Then the unit scans the fingerprints into its system, transforms them into a set of numbers, and sends them to a police computer system where they are stored.

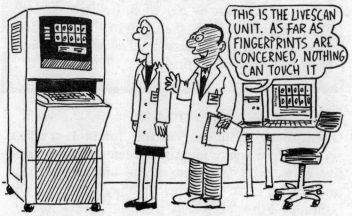

THIS IS THE LIVESCAN UNIT. AS FAR AS FINGERPRINTS ARE CONCERNED, NOTHING CAN TOUCH IT

Once an unidentified crime scene fingerprint has been fed into the police computer system, the system starts to search for similar prints in its database. The system delivers the closest matches it can find. Then an eagle-eyed fingerprint officer compares the crime scene print with those found by the computer to see if a match can be found. The sorts of things the fingerprint officer compares are the places where the lines of the fingerprint stop, start and divide.

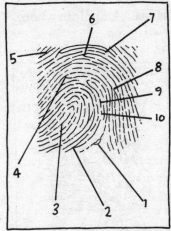

SCENE-OF-CRIME PRINT   COMPUTER-RECORDED PRINT

DIY detection: print puzzle

You're a detective investigating a break-in at a fish finger factory. You think it's the work of cat burglar Felix Frank ... but you need proof. The following unidentified fingerprint has been found at the factory. Does it match the print taken from Frank's police file?

FAINT PRINT FROM FISH
FINGER FACTORY

PRINT FROM FRANK'S FILE

Answer: Yes. There are at least 12 points where the prints match.

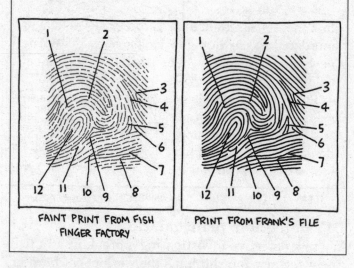

FAINT PRINT FROM FISH FINGER FACTORY

PRINT FROM FRANK'S FILE

Past times, past crimes

Computer-based fingerprint identification systems first came into use in about the early 1970s. Before that, fingerprints were recorded on cards and stored in box files; and the matching of crime scene fingerprints with those on file was done by hand. Not surprisingly, the arrival of computer-based fingerprint identification systems made the matching process easier and quicker. It also helped crack unsolved crimes from the past as well as from the present. In fact, in its first year of use, a computer-based fingerprint system helped the San Francisco Police Department in the USA solve 816 previously unsolved crimes. And that's just one police department in one part of one country!

True Crime Casebook
Case study 1: The Murder of Thora Rose

In 1963 a waitress named Thora Rose was found murdered in her home in Hollywood, USA. The news sent shock waves through the local community.

Police fingerprint files were not computerized in 1963. So, Hollywood detectives spent months looking at 30,000 box-filed fingerprints to see if they could find a match with the unidentified fingermarks

found at Thora Rose's home. But no match was found, and the hunt for the killer came to a halt.

For three decades the case remained unsolved. Then, in 1995, there was a break-through. By this time computerized fingerprint searches were all the rage. So detectives put the fingerprints found at Thora Rose's home through a computer to see if they could find a match.

And they did.

The killer's fingerprints hadn't been on file in 1963 because, at that time, he hadn't been arrested. However, over the following years, he'd been in and out of trouble with the law, and his fingerprints were on record for all to see.

Some 30 years after the murder of Thora Rose, her killer was finally put behind bars ... thanks to a high-tech fingerprint search.

Phoney fingerprints

Things that prove that a crime has been committed, or prove who committed it, are called evidence. Fingerprint evidence has helped kipper all sorts of criminals. But it isn't always as reliable as it's cracked up to be. On rare occasions, it has been faked, or forged, by crooked fingerprint officers in order to make a suspect appear guilty.

Here's how one dishonest dab dealer did just that: he photocopied one of the recorded fingerprints of the suspect. While the photocopied print was wet, he pressed some clear sticky-backed tape down on to it and lifted off the print.

Then he put the tape down on something taken from the crime scene and photographed the print with the tape left in place. When asked why he'd put tape on the print, he replied, "To protect it."

It was a cunning con-trick ... but not quite cunning enough. The dishonest dab dealer made one simple mistake. He forgot to destroy the fingerprint used to create his forgery. So, when a suspicious investigator decided to compare the forged print with all the suspect's prints on record, he found that the forged print matched one of the recorded prints perfectly. "So what?" I hear you ask. "Aren't prints taken from the same finger meant to be identical?" Well, no. Prints taken from the same finger will have the exact same pattern of swirling lines. But no two prints themselves should ever be exactly alike because no two prints are ever made using exactly the same amount of pressure, finger position, etc. When it was discovered that the forged print matched the one used to make the forgery, the finger of suspicion pointed at the dishonest dab dealer.

DNA IS A-OK!

The Files of Casey Cracked

Case: The Drunk Skunk burglary
Report number: 2

I was helping the fingerprint team dust The Drunk Skunk for dabs when the eyewitness walked in. She reckoned the two men she'd seen sneaking away from the bar matched the descriptions of Chip Cash and Louie Loan.

I'd heard of these guys: professional villains with criminal records as thick as telephone directories. I called my office and asked for their files to be biked over to the bar.

Criminal Record
Page 1 of 25

Name: Lewis "Louie" Loan
Date of birth: 27.10.1963
Occupation: Thief
Height: 6ft
Build: Thin as a blade
Eyes: Grey
Hair: Strawberry blond with copper streaks (dyed).

NOTES

Hobbies include collecting antiques, restoring old furniture, listening to classical music, thieving. Often wears a pink acrylic sweater and tartan trousers.

Criminal Record
Page 1 of 35

Name: Charles "Chip" Cash
Date of birth: 6.3.1961
Occupation: Thief
Height: 5ft 6ins
Build: Porky
Eyes: Sludge green
Hair: What hair?

NOTES

Suffers from constipation, flat feet, short sightedness, wind, nosebleeds, earache. Always wears the same "lucky" green underpants.

I poured myself a non-alcoholic beer. I knew Chip and Louie's fingerprints wouldn't be among those lifted from The Drunk Skunk. A quick glance at their police photos had told me that. I studied the crime scene again. I needed to find another type of clue that would link one or both of the suspects to the burgled bar.

It was then that I noticed a blood-flecked handkerchief lying behind the counter.

My heart started beating overtime. I knew that the bar's owner had cleaned up before he had locked up, so the handkerchief must have been dropped *after* he had gone to bed. Chip's file told me that he suffers from nosebleeds, so the blood on the hanky could have come from him. To find out for sure, I put the hanky into a clean specimen bag, labelled it with a tag, and sent it to the crime lab for urgent testing.

Finding a suspect's blood, spit, or other body bits at the scene of a crime can be as good as finding a fistful of useful fingerprints. That's because body bits are made up of cells, and each cell contains a molecule called DNA*. DNA holds a code that determines how you grow and what you look like. (Yep, that DNA sure has a *lot* to answer for!) Your DNA may be similar to that of your relatives, but unless you are an identical twin, it won't be exactly the same as anyone else's.

* The next time you're beaten at a general knowledge quiz or a game of Trivial Pursuit, ask the winner what DNA stands for. That'll wipe the smile off their face! The answer, by the way, is deoxyribonucleic (pronounced "dee-ox-ee-rye-bo-new-clay-ic") acid.

So far so good? OK. Here comes the crime-busting part. Forensic scientists (people who use science to help solve crimes) can extract a sample of DNA from a crime scene bloodstain, for example, and, using a chemical, chop it into different-sized pieces. These pieces are then separated in order of size in a jelly-like substance called agarose gel. This forms a pattern of dark bands that looks a bit like a supermarket bar code. This pattern is known as a DNA profile. If another DNA profile is developed using DNA taken from a suspect, the two profiles can be compared. If they match, you can bet your last box of bandages, the blood found at the crime scene came from the suspect. The technique for taking someone's DNA is known as DNA profiling.

As with fingerprints, DNA profiles of convicted criminals and people suspected of crimes are transformed into a set of numbers and stored on a national computer system. DNA profiles linked to unsolved crimes are stored on a computer system, too. The world's first national criminal intelligence database, the National DNA Database, was launched in the UK in 1995. It now holds over one million suspect and criminal profiles.

Past times, past crimes

DNA profiling was first used to catch a murderer in 1987. Since then, it has helped clear up all sorts of puzzles, including one of the twentieth century's most baffling mysteries.

True Crime Casebook
Case study 2: The Case of the Missing Princess

In 1920, a woman known as Anna Anderson appeared in Germany claiming to be Princess Anastasia, daughter of Czar Nicholas II of Russia. Czar Nicholas  and his family had been executed two years earlier, and it was thought that Anastasia had died along with her father.

Some believed Anna Anderson's claims – especially after the grave of the Russian royal family was opened, and the bones of Anastasia were nowhere to be found – but these claims were never proven. In 1964 Anna died, taking the truth of her identity to the grave.

Thirty years later, that truth finally became known. Before her death, Anna had had an operation, and some of her body tissue had been saved by the hospital. In 1994 this body tissue was subjected to DNA profiling. Then the DNA profile was compared with DNA profiles taken from direct descendants of the Russian royal family to see if there were any similarities. The findings were astounding. There were no similarities between Anna Anderson's DNA and that taken from the Czar's royal relatives. Anna Anderson had not been Princess Anastasia. She had been an ordinary woman who had managed to hoodwink many into believing that she was Russia's missing princess.

Crime-cracking fact
In 1993 Peter Hastings stabbed his girlfriend to death in her home in England. On discovering splashes of her blood on his shoes, he polished them, not realizing that he was sealing in tiny specks of blood. Over the next few years, huge advances were made in DNA profiling: and in 1999 those tiny spots of preserved blood were subjected to a new, improved DNA profiling method, which proved that the blood had come from Hastings's girlfriend ... and that he was her killer.

ON THE CLUE TRAIL

The Files of Casey Cracked

Case: The Drunk Skunk burglary
Report number: 3

Now, I ain't the gambling type. But I was willing to bet that the DNA extracted from the bloodstained handkerchief matched DNA taken from Chip Cash.

That just left Louie Loan. I needed proof that he, too, had been at the crime scene on the night of the burglary.

Then I remembered something I'd read in his criminal record.

Louie likes to wear a pink sweater made from acrylic. That got me thinking. We shed tiny broken bits of fibres from our clothes all the time. If Louie had rubbed up against anything at The Drunk Skunk, he'd have left some tiny fibres behind — unless he'd been naked, but I didn't want to go there.

I needed to find fabric fibres at the crime scene that matched clothing belonging to Louie. Crime scene fibres are generally under a millimetre long and finer than a human hair, so I knew they wouldn't be easy to find.

I headed straight for the window area where I *thought* they might have been dropped. Thousands of fibres can be picked up on windows that have been broken or forced open. If I could find fibres from Chip and Louie's clothing on The Drunk Skunk's smashed window, it would prove both crooks were in the bar when the crime was committed.

But how can Casey possibly collect such crucial fibres when they are too tiny to be seen? Here's another extract from *Crime-busting for Beginners* (unavailable from all good bookshops).

Crime-busting for Beginners

Fiddly fibre-collecting and testing
By Ivor Fluffy-Sweater

1. To collect fabric fibres from a crime scene, press some sticky-backed tape over the area where you think fibres might be found. Any fibres present will stick to the tape.

2. Stick the tape down on a clear plastic sheet. This will stop the fibres from getting lost and protect them from contamination.

3. Take your crime-scene fibres, together with some fibres from your suspect's clothing, down to a crime laboratory. Pop the crime-scene fibres under a microscope and weed out all those that aren't the same colour as the fibres taken from your suspect's clothing.

4. Using a high-powered comparison microscope, compare your suspect's fibres with the possible matches found at the crime scene. A comparison microscope lets you look at two pieces of evidence at the same time. It can magnify a fibre up to 400 times its normal size.

5. If both sets of fibres look the same colour, width, etc. under the microscope, check they really do match by carefully comparing their chemical make-up, and the dye that colours them.

Now, as luck would have it, the forensic scientists working on The Drunk Skunk case have had a break-through. They've proved that some of the fibres collected from the burgled bar came from a pink acrylic sweater. The only trouble is, there are thousands of pink acrylic sweaters like Louie Loan's on sale in the shops. How can the scientists prove that the crime scene fibres most likely came from Louie's sweater rather than from one of the thousands of similar sweaters on sale?

Because lots of batches of pink dye must have been used to colour the thousands of pink acrylic sweaters on sale, chances are no two batches would have been identical. If the scientists can prove that Louie's sweater and the fibres collected from The Drunk Skunk were coloured by the same batch of dye, it would narrow down the number of sweaters from which the crime scene fibres could have come. Put another way, it would rule out the possibility that The Drunk Skunk fibres could have come from one of the many pink acrylic sweaters coloured by slightly different batches of pink dye. From Louie Loan's point of view, this would be a dye-abolical discovery.

So, how can the scientists find out whether the crime scene fibres and those from Louie's sweater were coloured by the same batch of dye? By using a scientific technique called thin-layer chromatography, that's how. Thin-layer chromatography, or TLC for short, can be used to separate out the dye used to colour a bunch of man-made fibres so that you can see which chemicals make up the dye. Here's how TLC works:

1. The dyestuff is dissolved out of some crime scene fibres. Spots of the dye solution are put in a straight line along the lower edge of a slide coated with jelly-like stuff called silica gel.

2. The "spotted edge" of the slide is stood in a liquid called solvent, which rises up through the gel like water rises up through blotting paper.

3. As the solvent rises over the spots of dye, the different chemical components in the dye separate out at different rates, to form a line of dots.

4. If this process is repeated with dye taken from fibres found on a suspect's clothes, the two slides can be compared. If they match up, you can bet your last tie-dye T-shirt, the two sets of fibres were coloured by the same batch of dye.

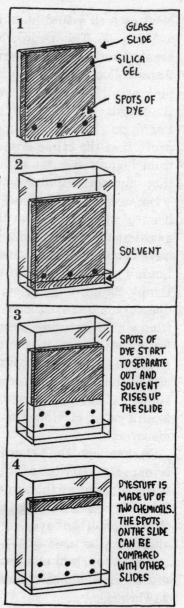

1
GLASS SLIDE
SILICA GEL
SPOTS OF DYE

2
SOLVENT

3
SPOTS OF DYE START TO SEPARATE OUT AND SOLVENT RISES UP THE SLIDE

4
DYESTUFF IS MADE UP OF TWO CHEMICALS. THE SPOTS ON THE SLIDE CAN BE COMPARED WITH OTHER SLIDES

The Files of Casey Cracked

Case: The Drunk Skunk burglary
Report number: 4

A call from the crime lab confirmed my suspicions. The fibres found at the bar matched those taken from Louie's pink acrylic sweater.

When the bar's cash till was eventually found, dumped empty on a nearby beach, it too had fabric fibres on it that matched Louie and Chip's clothing.

The crime lab team also discovered tiny splinters of glass in Chip and Louie's clothes that matched glass from the bar's broken window — proof that both men had been present at the break-in.

So, that was that. Case closed. All that was left was for me to pour myself a lemonade shandy, without the shandy, and try to figure out where I'd seen Louie Loan before.

Do you know where Casey has seen Louie Loan before? Clue: "in his police photo" is not the right answer!

Kippered by a carpet

Carpet fibres may not seem a big deal to you, but back in the early 1980s, these teeny threads helped unmask a murderer. Here's what happened.

True Crime Casebook
Case study 3: The Carpet Fibre Killings

From 1979–1981, in the city of Atlanta, Georgia, USA, a number of murdered bodies were found that had tiny yellow-green carpet fibres on them. The police suspected that the murderer, or murderers, had killed the victims on a yellow-green carpet and then dumped their bodies in the Chattahoochee River and elsewhere.

To confirm their suspicions, the police set a trap. They hid out by a bridge that crossed the Chattahoochee, and early one morning, they heard a loud splash. On the bridge, they spotted a car driven by a young man. The police questioned the driver, named Wayne Williams, and then let him go. They had no reason to arrest him because they had no proof that he had caused the splash by throwing a body into the river.

But that was soon to change.

Two days later, the body of a young man was found washed up not far from the bridge. In his hair was a single yellow-green fibre. Suddenly the police had reason to search Wayne Williams's home. When they stepped inside, they saw that the floors were covered with yellow-green carpet.

Having a yellow-green carpet made Wayne Williams look bad. But it didn't prove that he was a killer. For all the police knew, yellow-green carpets might have been all the rage in Atlanta in the 1970s. The fibres on the victims could have come from someone else's carpet.

But had they?

To find out, investigators traced the manufacturer of the yellow-green carpet and discovered how much of it had been sold in Georgia and the surrounding states. Working on the basis that this amount had  been evenly distributed throughout the Georgia area, they worked out how many homes in Atlanta were likely to have this type of carpet in one of their rooms. The answer was ... very few.

The carpet had only been on sale for 12 months, and it was reckoned that only one in nearly 8,000 homes in Atlanta were likely to have carpets like Wayne Williams's. In other words, the chance of the victims picking up the yellow-green fibres from anywhere other than Wayne Williams's home was low.

To make matters worse for Williams, detectives found purple fibres on some of the victims that matched the carpeting in his car. Investigators calculated that the chance of finding another car in Atlanta with the same purple carpeting was one in almost 4,000. In other words, the chance of the victims picking up the fibres from anywhere other than Williams's home and car was lower than an ant's IQ.

In February 1982 Wayne Williams was found guilty of murder.

"Take-away" clues

As you've probably sussed by now, criminals don't just leave clues at crime scenes. Often, they take away something that wasn't there when they arrived – remember the tiny splinters of window glass found in the clothes of The Drunk Skunk burglars?

Having chunks of crime scene glass in your clothes is obviously a tad suspicious. But what about ordinary things that we all get on our clothes from time to time, such as flower pollen, mud, sand or grass? Can these be proof of dodgy doings? Can anyone ever say for sure that a suspect definitely got grass on his clothes from one crime scene and not from anywhere else? The *True Crime Casebook* has the answer!

True Crime Casebook
Case study 4: The Planted Clue

On 2 November 1942 a man was out walking his dog in Central Park, New York, when suddenly he stumbled across the body of a woman. She had been strangled. By the looks of things, she had been murdered the previous day.

When a sharp-eyed scientist studied photos of the crime scene, he noticed that the woman's body was lying in a rare type of grass. Seeds of the same type of grass were later found in the pockets and trouser turn-ups of the 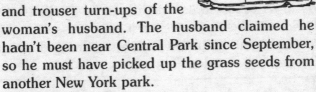 woman's husband. The husband claimed he hadn't been near Central Park since September, so he must have picked up the grass seeds from another New York park.

But had he?

A plant expert was put on the case. He told police that the only place in New York where the unusual type of grass grew was the hill in Central Park where the wife's body was discovered. The plant expert also said that the earliest this type of grass started to bloom was October.

So, the husband couldn't have picked up the grass seeds in September as he had claimed.

But he could have picked them up on 1 November.

In 1943 the husband was found guilty of his wife's murder and sentenced to die in the electric chair.

Different kinds of telltale print

If you think fingerprints are the only prints villains ever leave behind, think again! All sorts of prints and marks have helped lead police to criminals.

Trace that track!

Tyre tracks can reveal tonnes about the vehicle that made them, such as its size, the weight of its load, and the make of its tyres. Over time, tyres wear down; yet no two tyres wear down in exactly the same way. This means that if a getaway car is found before its tyres have been changed, the getaway tyres can be matched to their tracks. This would prove that the car was at the crime scene.

Like all bits of evidence, a crime scene tyre track has to be collected so that it can be studied later. Unlike small clues, however, it can't be sealed up in a clean bag and labelled with a tag. Instead, a copy of it has to be made.

Crime-busting for Beginners

How to make a copy of a tyre track
By Iona Sportscar

1. Mix some plaster with water in a strong plastic bag.
2. Cut off the corner of the bag and squeeze the plaster into the tyre track, in the same way that you'd pipe icing on to a cake, but without the fancy swirls – obviously!

3. Once the plaster has dried hard, pull up the cast and take it to a crime lab.

NB Use the same method to preserve shoeprints made in soft soil and bite-marks on food.

Crime-cracking fact
On 24 October 1983, Arthur Hutchinson broke into the home of the Laitner family in England and killed three members of the family. Detectives knew Hutchinson was lying when he said he hadn't ever been at the Laitner's house because bite-marks on cheese in their fridge matched his teeth exactly.

Shoe clues

Shoeprints can reveal loads about the people who made them, such as what kind of shoes they had on, how big or small their feet are, and which way they were heading. What's more, each of us walks slightly differently, which causes our shoes to wear down in a unique way. These signs of wear can be identified from our shoeprints.

Checking whether a suspect's shoe matches a print left at a crime scene is pretty straightforward: first a test print is made using the shoe. Then a plaster cast is made of the test print in the same way that a cast was made of the crime scene print. Finally, the two plaster casts are compared. If they are exactly the same, the suspect has some explaining to do.

DIY detection: the shoe-shop muggings

You're a detective investigating a string of attacks on shoe shops. The sole clue to the criminal's identity is a solitary shoeprint. A selection of shoes has been rounded up for questioning. It's up to you to spot which one left the telltale print. Can you do it?

48

THE TELLTALE PRINT...

THE USUAL SHOESPECTS

Answer: THE GUILTY SHOESPECT IS ... NUMBER SEVEN!

COBBLERS!

Crime-cracking fact
Would you believe that a print of your voice can be made? A voiceprint is a graph that shows how the strength of sound made by your voice changes as you speak.

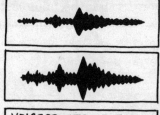

VOICEPRINTS OF TWO DIFFERENT PEOPLE SPEAKING THE SAME WORDS

If a bomber phones the police with a bomb warning, or a kidnapper calls to demand a ransom, the police can record the phone call. If a suspect is arrested a short while later, a voiceprint can be taken from the suspect and compared with the one produced from the recorded phone call. If the two voiceprints match, there's a good chance the suspect made the recorded phone call.

Telltale tool marks

A print or mark left by a screwdriver, chisel or other tool used to break open a window or door can lead to a burglar as surely as a shoeprint. Like tyres and shoe soles, tools get damaged and dented; yet no two tool blades get marked in exactly the same way. This means that if the tool that made a crime scene mark is found, and a forensic scientist uses it to make test marks, one of the test marks will match the crime scene mark perfectly.

Talking of tool marks, here's a true crime tale that just goes to show how even the most unlikely criminals can get caught in the end...

For 18 months, motorists in the south of Wales were pestered by an unknown vandal who liked scratching shocking swear words on to parked cars. The police thought the blame lay with a gang of yobs. But they were wrong. The vandal was an old lady. When police arrested her, they found tiny flakes of paint in her coat pocket, which forensic scientists confirmed matched paint from two of the vandalized cars. Police also found the knife she had used to scratch the cars, which had tiny bits of car paint inside its handle.

So, the next time your gran says she's been out for a walk, check her pockets!

BUSTED BY A BULLET

The study of guns and bullets is called ballistics. Crime-busters who specialize in dealing with gun crimes are sometimes called ballistics experts. By carefully examining the marks on a bullet found at a crime scene, a ballistics expert can link it to the gun from which it was fired. You see...

LADIES AND GENTLEMEN, BOYS AND GIRLS

Hey! What the...

WE INTERRUPT THIS BOOK TO BRING YOU A BULLET BULLETIN:

● The barrel of a gun has a spiral groove inside it that is designed to make a bullet spin. (Spinning bullets fire more accurately.)

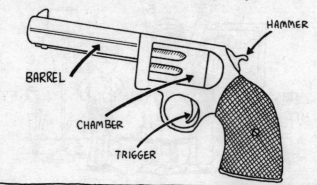

HAMMER

BARREL

CHAMBER

TRIGGER

● The spiral groove inside a gun's barrel cuts matching grooves into every bullet that whizzes through it.

BULLET

GROOVES, KNOWN AS RIFLING MARKS

● The grooves left on a fired bullet can help to trace the gun that fired it. That's because no two gun barrels are ever *exactly* alike.

● The factory tools used to make the barrel of a gun get worn down microscopically each time they're used. This means that if two brand-new guns, made in the same style in the same factory, are each fired once, the two bullets will have slightly different groove patterns. But if one of these guns is fired twice, both bullets will match.

● Over time, the barrel of a gun gets worn down; yet no two gun barrels wear down in exactly the same way. This is another reason why each gun leaves a unique pattern on the bullets it fires.

THIS IS THE END OF THE BULLET BULLETIN

Well, thank you very much. I was just about to say all that! Now, if I may continue … here's a tale of how one ballistics expert used his know-how to solve a baffling murder mystery.

True Crime Casebook
Case study 5: The Murder That Never Was

On 4 July 1989 a crowd of people gathered in a field in Illinois, USA, to celebrate American Independence Day. Without warning, one of the revellers fell off his deckchair, face first. Panic-stricken, his wife turned him over. On the right side of his chest she found a bullet wound. No one in the crowd had a gun; nor had anyone seen or heard anything suspicious. How or why the man had been shot was a complete mystery.

The fatal bullet was removed from the dead man's left lung and handed to a ballistics expert. Luckily, the bullet was in good shape because it hadn't hit anything hard like bone.

The ballistics expert carefully weighed and measured the bullet to find out what kind of gun it had come from. It turned out that it had come from a .44 magnum revolver. Lots of different gun manufacturers make this kind of weapon. So, the expert carefully examined the fatal bullet's pattern of grooves, and then checked a computer record of thousands of weapons to see if he could find the manufacturer with a pattern that matched. His search was a success. The murder weapon was a .44 Redhawk magnum revolver, made by a company called Ruger.

Straightaway the police visited local gun shops to see if anyone had sold such a revolver. But the search drew a blank. The murder weapon had probably been stolen or bought illegally.

The ballistics expert returned to the spot where the victim had sat. He placed a man-sized dummy in a deckchair, and inserted a long, thin wooden rod into its chest at the same angle that the bullet had entered the body.

By following the angle of the rod, the ballistics expert could trace the flight path of the bullet and see that it had come from a north-westerly direction.

That done, he next tried to work out the distance travelled by the bullet. Gun records told him that a bullet from a Ruger Redhawk magnum can hit an object up to 2.4 km away. However, the depth of the victim's gunshot wound suggested that the fatal bullet had probably travelled only about 450–640 m before it had struck. That meant that the murder weapon had probably been fired from a spot 450–640 m north-west of the field. Armed with this information, police visited every house within that firing range until they came across a crucial clue.

Outside one of the houses, police found a metal oil drum riddled with holes. Nearby lay the bullets that had made those holes. Using a comparison microscope, the ballistic expert compared one of these bullets with the one taken from the dead man's lung. The two bullets matched, which proved that they had both been fired from the same gun.

The police were sure that the gun's owner lived in the house with the oil drum. But before they could get a search warrant, they needed to know one thing: could a bullet really travel the 450–640 m from the house to the field without hitting any of the trees or buildings in between?

Guessing that the fatal bullet had been fired upwards, the ballistics expert drew a diagram of the path it had probably travelled. His drawing showed that the bullet could indeed have missed all the obstacles in between the house and the field. (When a bullet is fired upwards, it follows a curved path.)

Now the police had all the evidence they needed to search the house. Inside, they found the murder weapon, its owner, and the answer to the mystery.

On the day of the killing the gun's owner had been shooting at a jug on top of the oil drum to improve his aim. After firing five shots, he'd given the gun to his girlfriend so that she could have a go. But she had tilted the gun too high and missed the target by miles. It was this stray shot that had killed the man in the field. His death hadn't been a deliberate murder as first thought. It had been an awful, awful accident.

Bullet casings

It's not just the business end of a bullet that can snare a shooter. The casing that holds the bullet can help collar a crook, too.

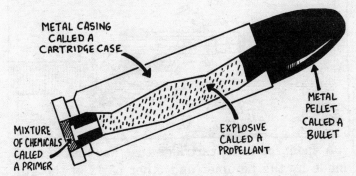

METAL CASING CALLED A CARTRIDGE CASE

MIXTURE OF CHEMICALS CALLED A PRIMER

EXPLOSIVE CALLED A PROPELLANT

METAL PELLET CALLED A BULLET

Here's what happens when a gun is fired:

As the trigger is pulled, a hammer inside the gun hits the back of the cartridge case and ignites the primer. The primer ignites the propellant, and the force created by the burning propellant pushes the bullet out of the gun.

With revolvers, the cartridge case of a fired bullet stays inside the gun until the gun is reloaded by hand.

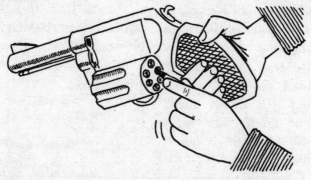

Automatic pistols automatically chuck out a cartridge case every time the gun is fired. (That's why they're called automatics.)

A spent, or used, cartridge case has marks on it made by the hammer and other parts of the gun from which it was ejected. These marks help ballistics experts work out what type of gun the cartridge case came from.

Incredible IBIS

Matching a crime scene bullet to the gun that fired it is all very fine. But suppose the bullet you've got comes from a crime committed long ago, and the suspect weapon was never found? This is where a system like IBIS comes to the rescue. IBIS stands for Integrated Ballistic Indentification System (try saying that with a mouth full of popcorn!). It's a sophisticated computer linked up to a microscope and two tiny video cameras. Here's how it works:

1. A crime scene bullet is placed under one of the cameras and filmed from every angle.

2. A highly magnified image of the bullet appears on the computer's screen.

3. The image is scanned into the computer, which searches through its database looking for other images that match.

4. If a match is found, it proves that the bullet came from one of the guns police have confiscated from known or suspected villains. This links the gun's owner to the unsolved crime.

The beauty of IBIS is that it can match bullets from past crimes to recently confiscated guns in less time than it takes to go to the loo. In under a minute, it can compare an actual bullet with thousands of others in its database. To try and do this by hand would take years.

Hands up! Who's been handling my gun?

Would you believe that there's a simple test that can tell you whether or not someone has fired a gun within the last few hours? When a handgun is fired, it leaves traces of metals from inside the gun on the shooter's face, hand, hair and clothes. If the shooter is tracked down quickly enough, this gunpowder-residue can be collected by wiping his or her hands with cotton wool dipped in a weak solution of acid. Gunpowder residue testing is especially useful when it comes to figuring out whether a corpse found holding a fired gun had the gun placed in its hand after death.

BLASTS AND BOMBS

You don't need to be a bright spark to know that an explosion is bad news. But you do need to have your brain wired up correctly to be able to tell whether an explosion was caused accidentally (say, by a gas leak) or deliberately (say, by a bomb).

Bits and bombs

Explosion investigators can discover the cause of a blast by studying the wreckage left behind. Suppose a car has exploded and the force of the explosion has sent bits of the car flying into the walls of a nearby shed. The investigators could work out how fast the bits were travelling by measuring how deeply they were embedded in the shed's walls. If the bits were travelling at 1,000–8,500 m per second, the car was probably blown up by a high explosive such as TNT or dynamite.

Other bomb clues that explosives experts look out for include:

● the distinctive burning or melting marks that an exploding bomb leaves on the things closest to it

● traces of the explosive used in the bomb
● bits of the container that held the explosive.

You'd think it would, wouldn't you? But it doesn't. In fact, quite a lot of a bomb can be left behind after a blast. In 1985 agents investigating a car bombing in Florida, USA, found tiny bits of the metal pipe that had contained the explosive. They also found fragments of the two end caps used to stop the explosive spilling out of the pipe. Luckily, part of the manufacturer's mark was stamped on each cap. This made it easier for the police to trace the caps back to the store that had sold them ... and from there on to the bomber who had bought them.

On 12 October 1984 a bomb blast tore through a hotel in Brighton, England. The bomb had been designed to assassinate the British Prime Minister who was staying at the hotel. But it missed its target and killed other hotel guests instead. From one of the dead bodies investigators recovered an unfamiliar metal speck, about the size of a pinhead. When forensic scientists scrutinized this speck, they discovered it was part of an electrical circuit board. This told the scientists that the bomb had been timed to go off by an electronic timer, which could have been set six months before the blast.

Bombs in the sky

With airplane bombings, crash investigators often try to pinpoint *where* the explosion took place because if they can find out in whose suitcase the bomb was planted, they're halfway to finding out who was behind the blast. This kind of sleuthing is mind-bogglingly tricky, as those who investigated the bombing of Pan Am Flight 103 know only too well. Here's what happened:

True Crime Casebook

Case study 6: The Bombing of Pan Am Flight 103

On 21 December **1988** Pan Am flight **103** was flying over the Scottish town of Lockerbie when disaster struck: a blast blew the plane right out of the sky. The pieces of the plane hurtled to the ground; a great ball of fire erupted; and **270** people died.

The crash investigators working on the case were sure the blast was the work of a bomber, but they needed to know exactly where the explosion had taken place. So, teams of investigators and local police gathered up the remains of the plane (which had been shattered and scattered over *845* square miles of southern Scotland and northern England). Then technicians began to rebuild the plane inside a huge aircraft hangar, to try to find out how it had broken apart.

After months of long, hard work, most of the aircraft was rebuilt. Only the section of the plane containing the forward luggage compartment couldn't be found. From this, investigators deduced that the blast had most probably been caused by a bomb planted in one of the suitcases that had been housed in the missing luggage compartment.

A careful examination of the bits of baggage found in the wreckage revealed that one of the blasted suitcases had traces of chemicals in it. Back at the crime lab, scientists identified the chemicals as PETN and RDX – both of which are found in a high explosive called Semtex, which is often used by terrorists.

The investigating team were now convinced that the Semtex-stained suitcase was the one in which the bomb had been packed. But to whom had the suspicious suitcase belonged?

A luggage transfer computer record suggested that the suitcase had been checked in at an airport in Malta, and later loaded on to Pan Am flight 103. But the record didn't say who the owner was. To answer that question, scientists studied the thousands of scraps of fabric that had been collected from the crash scene. Among them, they found a few stained with traces of Semtex. Clearly, these bits of clothing had been extremely close to the bomb. More likely than not, they had been packed around it to stop it rattling about in the suitcase.

One of the Semtex-stained scraps had come from a baby's jumpsuit. On it was the label of a shop in Malta. When police traced the scrap back to the Maltese shop, they found that the shopkeeper clearly remembered selling the jumpsuit and the other pieces of Semtex-stained clothing to one particular customer. The reason this particular customer had stuck in the shopkeeper's mind was he hadn't paid any attention to the sizes or styles of the clothes he was buying.

The customer quickly became a prime suspect; and in time, he was tracked down, tried in a court of law and found guilty of the fateful bombing.

DOCUMENT DETECTION

Did you know that during your teens your handwriting will develop a more mature style? By the time you're an adult, this new sophisticated style will be fully developed and will remain more or less the same until you are old and grey. All adults have their own individual style of handwriting, which can be used to identify them. One reason everyone's writing is slightly different is that each letter of the alphabet can be written in lots of ways. To see for yourself, check out how these two writers have formed the letters "a", "B" and "p".

Dear Mrs Brown
If you want
to see your son
again, you've got
to pay me
£1 million

A. Kidnapper

Dear A Kidnapper,

If you want your £1 million, you've got to keep him.

Mrs Brown

Who wrote this ransom note?

Document examiners are trained to be able to prove whether such and such a person wrote a particular letter, note or document. Say a kidnapper has disguised his handwriting on a ransom note so brilliantly it looks totally unlike his usual handwriting. By carefully comparing the writing on the ransom note with samples of the kidnapper's usual handwriting, a document examiner would be able to spot a similar style to both types of handwriting. This would prove they were written by the same person. The sort of things a document examiner looks out for when comparing handwritings are the slant, height and shape of the letters, and the ways in which each letter stops and starts. Genuine handwriting uses smooth, flowing pen strokes. Disguised handwriting often includes clumsy pen strokes, with letters stopping or starting awkwardly, and the same letter being formed in an odd or different way each time it is written. To a document examiner, all this spells "suspicious".

Warning: Document examiners can also tell if someone has tried to copy someone else's handwriting, so bear this in mind the next time you plan to fake a sick note from your mum or dad!

Investigating ink

Careful examination of the ink used to write a document can help to expose a forgery, too.

Suppose you wrote a friend a cheque for £1 using black ink, and the swindling swine added a string of noughts to the amount, using a different make of black ink.

Back at a crime lab, a document examiner would be able to prove the cheque had been written with different inks by examining it under infrared rays and blue-green lighting. Under this special kind of lighting, some of the dyes in the inks would emit, or give out, infrared rays; others would absorb them. Because the two inks are different makes, they are not made up of the exact same dyes; therefore, the amounts of infrared emitted by each ink would be different. This would prove that two separate inks were used on the cheque. Even if your friend had written those extra noughts with a similar pen to yours, made by the same manufacturer, chances are it wouldn't have been filled with ink from the exact same batch as yours, so there'd still be identifiable differences between the two inks.

Crime-cracking fact
Like bank notes, many official documents have hidden security marks that can only be seen under a type of light called ultraviolet, or UV. When viewed under UV, these security marks fluoresce, or glow like a luminous watch-face glows in the dark.

TLC to the rescue

Remember thin-layer chromatography, or TLC for short? (Check out page 39 if you don't.) If a document examiner carefully removes a tiny drop of ink from a handwritten letter, she or he can use TLC to separate out the chemicals that make up the ink. Once the examiner knows the chemical make-up of the ink, she or he can compare it with the chemical composition of other known inks to try to find a match. To help with comparisons, there is an International Ink Library in the USA which keeps information about thousands of writing inks.

Magic writing

Have you ever noticed how when you write really heavily on the top page of a writing pad, an impression of what you wrote appears on the page, or pages, underneath? A piece of equipment called electrostatic detection apparatus can show up handwriting impressions that are too faint to be seen normally. Here's how this electrostatic detection apparatus, or ESDA, works:

1. The page with the handwriting impressions is placed on top of the apparatus, and sucked down by an air pump, to hold it in place. A film of thin plastic is then pulled tightly across the page.

PLASTIC

DOCUMENT

71

2. An electrical charge is passed over the page, which collects in the invisible handwriting impressions.

3. The page is coated with a fine black powdered ink that sticks to the electrostatically charged impressions. This produces a copy of the invisible words on the thin film of plastic.

ESDA can also be used to show whether a letter was altered after it had been written and torn off a writing pad. If the ESDA test reveals differences between the letter and the handwriting impressions left behind on the writing pad, you can bet your bottom banana the letter has been altered.

Dodgy diaries

Document examiners have exposed some pretty foxy frauds in their time, but one of the most daring document con tricks ever cracked involved the diaries of Adolf Hitler. (For those of you who have skipped a few history lessons, Adolf Hitler was the German chap with the toothbrush moustache and dodgy hair who started World War II.)

In 1981 a West German magazine company announced the find of the century: they had just been handed the personal diaries of Adolf Hitler.

Publishers across the globe couldn't wait to read the diaries, and mountains of money were offered for permission to publish them worldwide.

But in 1983 the diaries were proved to be fake.

When document examiners viewed them under ultraviolet light, they discovered that the paper on which they had been written contained a paper-whitening substance that hadn't come into use until after Hitler's death in 1945! They also discovered that the bindings of the diaries were made from modern products; and that none of the different inks used to write the diaries had been widely used while Hitler was alive.

The greatest find of the century was, in fact, the century's biggest fraud.

CORPSE CLUES

Dead men can't talk; but their corpses can "speak volumes" about how and when they died. Even if all that is left of a murdered man is his skeleton, crime-busters can still work out who the man was ... and who killed him.

Time of death

A forensic pathologist is someone who examines bodies that have died unexpectedly or in dodgy circumstances, to find out how they died and how long they've been dead. Knowing approximately when a person died can be crucial in a murder case because it can rule out one suspect and cast suspicion on another. If Joe Bloggs can prove that he wasn't at the crime scene at the time the murder is thought to have taken place, it lets him off the hook; but if he can't prove that he wasn't at the crime scene at the time the murder is thought to have been committed, he could be a suspect.

I COULD NOT HAVE DONE IT, I WAS AT MY ... UH ... FLOWER - ARRANGING CLASS

Deduction by degree

After death, a body goes through all sorts of weird changes. These include a stiffening of the muscles and a drop in body temperature.* To estimate the

---

* In extreme climates, such as in central Australia, the body temperature after death may rise.

74

time of death, a forensic pathologist has to study all these "after death changes" very carefully.

Let's start with the drop in body temperature. Did you know that the normal temperature of a living, breathing body is 37°C? In countries with climates that are neither very hot nor very cold, like the UK, a person's body temperature usually drops after death at an average rate of 1°C per hour. If a forensic pathologist gets to a body within the first 12–18 hours after death, he or she can record the temperature of the corpse at regular intervals, and so begin to estimate how long ago death occurred. This may sound straightforward, but the pathologist also has to take into account things that can affect the cooling rate such as the temperature the body has been exposed to, and its size (a fat person cools more slowly than a thin one).

To measure the temperature of a corpse, a forensic pathologist either **a)** makes a cut near the ribs and sticks a special thermometer into the wound, or **b)** inserts the thermometer up the corpse's bottom.

ER... I THINK I'M FEELING BETTER NOW!

POLICE LINE DO CROSS POL

Stiff as a ... stiff

Ever wondered why a dead body sometimes gets called a stiff? It's because, after death, a body's muscles usually relax completely, and then stiffen up. This stiffening starts in the face, and generally takes up to 12 hours to spread over the entire body,

75

before gradually going away. In countries where the weather gets neither very hot nor very cold, the stiffness usually starts to disappear about 36–48 hours after death. (In hot places, it starts and disappears faster; in cold places, it starts faster, but disappears more slowly.)

I DON'T KNOW IF HE IS A STIFF, OR JUST BORED STIFF

PARTY POLITICAL BROADCAST

Forensic pathologists can use the amount of stiffness as a guide to help them estimate when death struck. Again, the speed at which the stiffness starts and spreads can be affected by all sorts of things, such as the surrounding air temperature, so the pathologist has to take these things into account.

Because establishing time of death is tricky, detectives always keep a look out for other clues to back up a pathologist's findings:

DIY detection: time for murder

It's two o'clock in the morning and you're a detective at a murder scene. The victim has been hit over the head with a hammer. You're about to ask the forensic pathologist to give a very rough estimate of the time of death when suddenly you spot something at the crime scene that might answer your question.

At what time do you reckon the victim was bumped off?

77

Answer: The likely time of death is around 10.30 pm – the time shown on the murder victim's shattered and stopped wristwatch. The watch may have got broken (and stopped working) during a struggle, or when the victim tried to ward off a blow to his head.

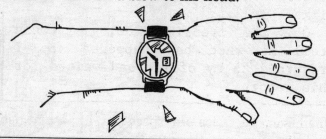

Cause of death

You don't need to be a pathologist to know whether someone has died unexpectedly or not. But that doesn't mean it's always easy to tell whether a murder has been committed. Just take a look at this report from the files of Casey Cracked:

The Files of Casey Cracked

Case: Chip Cash cashes in his chips
Report number: 1

Chip Cash had about as much charm as a postbox. So when I got a call saying that he had been found dead, I didn't send a Get Well card. But I did stroll down to the crime scene.

Chip was lying sprawled out, face down, at the bottom of some stairs.

The cause of his death wasn't clear. He could've fallen down the stairs by accident, or he might've been pushed. Perhaps he'd been bumped off elsewhere and his lifeless body placed near the stairs to make it look like a fall.

Only the forensic pathologist could tell me what had happened. So I returned to my office and waited for his report.

When someone dies unexpectedly, a pathologist carefully examines the corpse for clues that will reveal whether the person died naturally or by accident, suicide, or murder. This kind of body examination is called a "post mortem" or an "autopsy".

Crime-busting for Beginners

Post mortems
By Dr Ben D Bone

NB Remember to make notes and take photographs of all findings as you work.

1. Put on protective clothing and a face mask.
2. Examine the outside of the body carefully. Keep an eye open for marks such as bruises, pricks from injection

needles, wounds on the arms and hands which might show the dead person tried to ward off an attacker.

3. Weigh and measure the body.

4. Cut open the body and remove the important organs such as the lungs, heart, brain and liver. Inspect everything carefully for signs of anything suspicious.

5. Remove the stomach contents and send them to a lab for closer inspection.

6. Collect samples of skin, hair, blood or anything else that needs closer examination and send them to the lab.

7. At the end, put the insides back in the body and sew it up.

8. Have lunch (optional).

LUNCH MENU
• LIVER
• KIDNEYS
• TONGUE
• RIBS

There are a great many things that a good pathologist, like myself, can deduce, or work out, by examining a body. For example:

Evidence	Deduction
1. No soot found in the lungs of a body dragged out of a fire. 	The person was probably dead before the fire began. (Soot is drawn into the lungs by breathing.) The fire may have been started deliberately to get rid of the body.
2. Foaming from the mouth and nose, plus lots of microscopic water organisms called diatoms found in the lungs and kidneys.	The deceased died by drowning. (Large numbers of diatoms are drawn into the body by breathing.) If only a few diatoms had been found, the body was probably dead when it entered the water.
3. When viewed under a microscope, white blood cells can be seen around the edges of a wound. 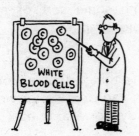	The wound was made when the person was alive. (White blood cells rush to a wound to help fight infection.) If no white blood cells had been found, the wound had to have been made after death, i.e. after the heart had stopped pumping blood around the body.

4. Smell of bitter almonds coming from a body, plus a bright pink patch on the lowest part of the body.

The person was poisoned with cyanide. After death, a person's blood sinks to the lowest part of their body. It then seeps out of the blood vessels and into the surrounding tissue, leaving a dark purple or reddish-purple patch on the skin. If this patch is an unusual colour, poison may have been the cause of death.

5. Injury to the scalp, fractured skull and damage to the part of the brain immediately beneath the fracture.

The victim was hit over the head with something heavy. (If the victim had fallen and hit his head, the damage to the brain would have been found on the opposite side to the scalp injury and fracture.)

6. Bruising to the throat and a groove around the neck.

The victim was strangled with some sort of tie, cord, strap, etc.

The Files of Casey Cracked

Case: Chip Cash cashes in his chips
Report number: 2

The forensic pathologist was not a guy who liked to linger.

"Chip Cash died of manual strangulation," he announced as he dropped his post mortem report on my desk, and headed for the door.

"Whoa! Wait up doc!" I called as he sped off down the corridor. "Are you sure?"

"Yes," he shouted, still on the move. "One particular bone and some cartilage in his neck were crushed, and there were hand-shaped bruises on his throat — all clear signs of manual strangulation."

"But I didn't notice any bruising on his neck," I shouted, trying to catch up.

"That's because, in this particular case, the bruising was on the layers of flesh under his skin."

The doc stopped suddenly, and held up a photo of a cut-open neck. On the layers of flesh inside the skin, I could see some deep purplish hand-marks. Perhaps the hand-shaped bruises usually seen on the surface of a strangled neck had faded.

"Had Chip's dead body been moved?" I asked, slowly regaining my breath.

"Most definitely. Chip Cash was found lying on his front with purple patches on his back."

I looked at the doc blankly.

"Remember those dark purple patches that appear on the lowest parts of a body after death? Well, after a while, they become 'fixed'. In other words, if somebody dies lying on their back, the purple patches will be 'fixed' on the back of the body. But if a body is found lying on its front, with purple patches on its back…"

"…the body must have been moved after death."

"Exactly."

And so saying, the doc sped off, leaving me with a stitch in my side … and a murder on my hands.

Identifying the body

Trying to conceal a murder by making it look like an accident is risky. So too is trying to conceal a murder by destroying the body. Below are just some of the methods the world's most infamous killers have used to hide their crimes: and in all these cases, the victims' bodies were identified and the murderers caught.

- PROFESSOR JOHN WEBSTER
- 1849, MASSACHUSETTS, USA
- BURNED HIS VICTIM'S BODY IN A LABORATORY OVEN

- JOHN HAIGH
- 1949, WEST SUSSEX, ENGLAND
- DISSOLVED HIS VICTIM IN A VAT OF ACID

- ISSEI SAGAWA
- 1981, PARIS, FRANCE
- ATE SOME OF HIS VICTIM'S DEAD BODY AND HID THE REMAINING PORTIONS IN TWO SUITCASES

- DENNIS NILSEN
- 1983, LONDON, ENGLAND
- CUT UP HIS MANY VICTIMS AND BOILED SOME OF THEIR BODY PARTS IN A SAUCEPAN

Identifying a body may not be your idea of cool crime-busting, yet it is one of the most important parts of a murder investigation because the naming of a corpse often leads to the naming of a killer. Even if only a skeleton remains, useful deductions can still be made about what type of person that skeleton belonged to. For example:

● The size and shape of a skull or pelvis can reveal the sex of a person. The pelvis of a man is much narrower than that of a woman.

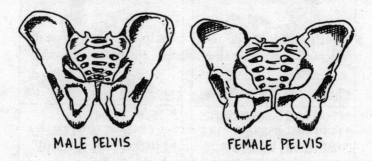

MALE PELVIS   FEMALE PELVIS

● The shape of an eye socket and a nose hole can reveal a person's race. In European people, the top of the nose is usually narrow: in African and Asian people, it tends to be broader.

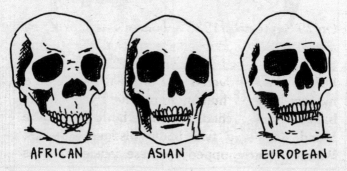

AFRICAN   ASIAN   EUROPEAN

- The length of the arm or leg bones can be used to work out the height of a dead person. There is a link between the length of a person's limbs and their total height.

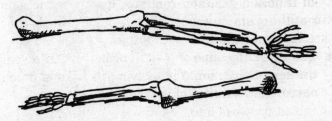

- Teeth can often be used to help work out a dead person's age, particularly if that person died young. Bodies can sometimes be identified from records held by dentists, too.

One of the most famous murder cases involving the identification of body bits and bones took place in 1935.

True Crime Casebook
Case study 7: The Mystery of the Headless Corpses

On 29 September 1935 a woman was walking by a river in Scotland when she spotted a scattering of parcels washed up on the river's bank. To her horror, she discovered one of them contained a maggot-infested human arm. The river and its banks were searched, and more body parts were found, including two badly disfigured heads. Whoever had chopped up these faceless bodies had taken a lot of trouble to make sure they couldn't be named or traced to their homes.

The recovered body bits were sent to a team of pathologists. The pathologists were pretty sure the bits belonged to two bodies only. So, they assembled the mixed-up parts into what looked like two human shapes. Careful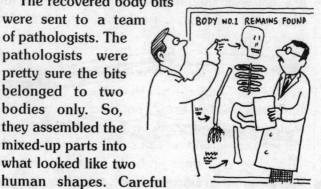

study of the bones told them that one of the victims was a woman aged about 20. The other was a woman aged between 35–45.

Meanwhile, the police were cracking on with their investigation. One of the recovered body parts had been wrapped in a piece of newspaper dated 15 September. This suggested that the bodies had been dumped on or just after that date. Another body bit was found wrapped in a  local newspaper, again dated 15 September, which had only been sold in the Morecambe and Lancaster areas of England, south of where the washed-up body parts were found.

By chance, the police discovered that

two women had disappeared from Lancaster around about the same date. One of them was a 20-year-old maid named Mary Jane Rogerson. The other was her 34-year-old employer, Mrs Isabella Ruxton.

It was now up to the pathologists to find out whether the bodies were those of Mrs Ruxton and her maid. They knew that Mary had had a birthmark on her arm. They had also been told that she had had scars on her thumb and belly. Yet they could find no signs of these marks on the younger body. However, they did find evidence that the skin had been scraped away in the places where these marks would have been. This suggested that the killer had known that these marks might identify the body and had got rid of them.

One thing the killer hadn't got rid of, however, was the fingerprints. When fingerprints were taken from one of the hands, they were found to match prints on Mary Jane Rogerson's possessions. At last, the police had proof that one of the bodies was that of Mary Jane Rogerson.

The pathologists now turned their attention to the second body. Photographs of Mrs Ruxton when she was alive showed that she had unusual prominent teeth and a big nose. Both of these easily recognizable features had been removed from the second body. So too had its fingerprints.

This prompted the pathologist to try something no one had ever done before.

They placed a negative photograph of the second skull over a photo of Mrs Ruxton's head to see if it would match. And it did. Perfectly. (Nowadays this technique is carried out using a video camera.) There was no doubt that the second body belonged to Mrs Ruxton.

A PHOTO OF THE SECOND SKULL IS PLACED OVER A PHOTO OF THE MISSING MRS RUXTON

Now all the pathologists had to do was to find out the cause of death. Mary's body was too badly damaged to be able to tell how she had died. But a careful examination of Mrs Ruxton's body revealed that one particular bone and two particular cartilages in her neck were broken – a clear sign that she had been strangled.

But by whom?

When police searched the home of Mrs Ruxton and her doctor husband, they found traces of human fat in the drains. They also found plenty of bloodstains, despite signs of a clean up. The team of pathologists had suspected that someone with medical know-how had cut up Mrs Ruxton and her maid, and they were right. On 5 November 1935, Dr Ruxton was sentenced to death by hanging. Before he died, he confessed to killing his wife in a fit of fury. He also confessed to strangling Mary because she had witnessed the murder of his wife.

How time flies!

One reason the Ruxton murder case is famous in crime-busting circles is that it was one of the first cases in which insects were used to help pinpoint the time of death.

The minute flies get the whiff of a corpse, which doesn't take long, they're all over it, laying eggs.* The eggs hatch 12–15 hours later, and the tiny maggots start feeding on the rotting flesh. The wriggling maggots grow and grow, then curl up in a pupa case before hatching into flies. The time it takes for an egg to develop into a maggot and then into a fully fledged fly is well known. This means that insect experts called entomologists can look to see what stage the biggest maggots on a corpse have reached, and then count back the days to when the first eggs must have been laid. From this, they can estimate the time of death.

THERE'S BEEN A MURDER. QUICK, LET'S FLY...

The rate at which maggots grow varies with the surrounding air temperature. So an entomologist leaves temperature-recording instruments at the crime scene for up to a week. These instruments automatically record the temperature changes that

* If you've just eaten, you may want to read this section later. If you've thrown up what you've just eaten, you may as well carry on reading.

the maggots were exposed to. Once the entomologist knows the sort of temperatures the maggots experienced, she or he can age them to within hours.

Crime-cracking fact

In 2002 an American company began selling tiny microchips that can be injected into your arm and used to identify you. Each microchip stores a number on it, which can be read by a hand-held electronic scanner. Once "read", the number can be used to access personal information about you stored on a secure database. These microchips could be used to identify all sorts of people including accident or murder victims who wind up dead far from home.

DEADLY DOSES

For most of history, poisoners have been able to bump off their nearest and dearest confident that they were unlikely to get caught because no one knew how to detect poisons. Those who did get rumbled often only had themselves to blame because they'd done something incredibly careless, such as confide in a blabbermouth. Take the case of Frances Howard, Countess of Somerset, for example:

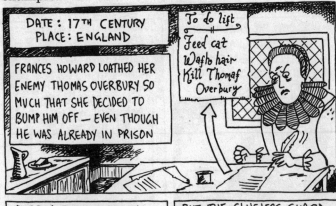

DATE: 17TH CENTURY
PLACE: ENGLAND

FRANCES HOWARD LOATHED HER ENEMY THOMAS OVERBURY SO MUCH THAT SHE DECIDED TO BUMP HIM OFF — EVEN THOUGH HE WAS ALREADY IN PRISON

To do list
Feed cat
Wash hair
Kill Thomas Overbury

ONE DAY, FRANCES PAID A GUARD TO POISON HIS FOOD

BUT THE CLUELESS GUARD GOT CAUGHT RED-HANDED AND OVERBURY LIVED ON...

PRISON MENU
BREAD AND WATER
CABBAGE SOUP
POISON

UNDAUNTED, FRANCES BRIBED THE PRISON DOCTOR'S ASSISTANT TO ADMINISTER THE POISON AS A MEDICINE

THIS TIME HER PLAN WORKED, OVERBURY KICKED THE BUCKET AND NO ONE SUSPECTED A THING. UNTIL ...

... ONE DAY, THE PRISON DOCTOR'S ASSISTANT FELL GRAVELY ILL AND, FEELING HE MIGHT DIE A SINNER, TOLD OF HIS GUILTY SECRET

SUDDENLY, IT WAS ALL OVER FOR FRANCES

BAH! I WOULD'VE GOTTEN AWAY WITH IT TOO, IF IT HADN'T BEEN FOR THAT PESKY, MEDDLING PRISON DOCTOR'S ASSISTANT...

HER CAREER OF CRIME WAS AT AN END!

Thankfully, the days when you could mash a deadly dose of poison into someone's cornflakes and be sure of getting away with it are over. Nowadays poison experts called toxicologists are incredibly clued-up when it comes to detecting poisons. They can test a sample of a victim's blood (or pee or other body bits) to see whether it contains poison, and, if so, what type of poison it contains. They can even identify a poison if only the tiniest trace is found in a victim's body. In short, poison is rarely used as a means of murder these days because it is no longer the untraceable killer it once was. You only have to check out *Crime-busting for Beginners* to see the sort of scientific sleuthing the modern-day poisoner is up against.

Crime-busting for Beginners

How to extract poison from a body
By Justin Casey-Lives

1. Find someone who you think may have been poisoned. Telltale signs include:
● stomach pains
● shakiness
● feeling sick
● being sick
● diarrhoea
● constipation
● collapse
● death
2. Ask for a sample of the victim's blood. Pop the blood in a test tube. Add a special liquid called an extracting solvent, and stick a stopper in the test tube.
3. Put the test tube in a high-speed micro centrifuge and turn the centrifuge on. (A centrifuge is a machine that whizzes round

and round at high speeds in order to separate substances of different densities.)

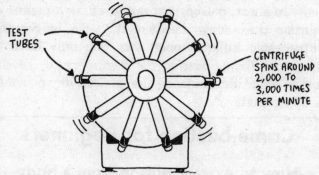

TEST TUBES

CENTRIFUGE SPINS AROUND 2,000 TO 3,000 TIMES PER MINUTE

4. As the centrifuge spins round, the extracting solvent will absorb anything that shouldn't be in the blood, such as poison, and rise to the top of the test tube. The heavier blood will sink to the bottom.

5. Test the solvent to see what type of poison it contains. Toxicologists generally identify an unknown poison by first splitting it up into the substances from which it is made. To do this they use various scientific techniques including chromatography (see page 39).

The Seattle cyanide murders

Although poison is no longer the popular means of murder it once was, there are always a few people who think they can give the scientific sleuths the slip, and get away with the perfect poisoning.

True Crime Casebook
Case study 8: The Seattle Cyanide Murders

On 11 June 1986, a woman in Seattle, Washington, USA, woke up with a raging headache. She took two capsules of a painkiller called Excedrin to cure the pain. Within hours she was dead.

When toxicologists tested the powder in the capsules, they found it contained cyanide. When the woman's blood was tested, it too was found to contain cyanide. It looked like someone had deliberately opened up the capsules, emptied the medicinal powder out into a bowl, added some cyanide, mixed the whole lot together, and put the mixture back in the capsules.

To be on the safe side, thousands of bottles of Excedrin capsules were taken off shop shelves across America and checked to see whether they too were contaminated with cyanide. The check uncovered two more poison-packed bottles – both of which had been found in shops in Seattle.

On 17 June the police got a call from a Seattle grandmother named Stella Nickell. She said that her husband, Bruce, had died 11 days earlier after taking two Excedrin capsules. A sample of

Bruce's blood was tested and found to contain cyanide. So too did the two bottles of Excedrin found in the Nickells' home.

The case bore all the signs of a product-tampering scare. At first, police suspected that the tampering might have been the work of a terrorist, a mad person, or someone angry with the makers of Excedrin. But strangely, no one telephoned to take credit for the crime or to ask for money to stop the tampering.

Meanwhile, a chemist working at an FBI crime lab made a startling discovery: all the cyanide-laced capsules contained tiny crystal-like specks of green. When these green specks were examined on a complex scientific instrument called a mass spectrometer, they were found to be made up of four common chemicals. Using a computer programme that lists the chemical make-up of thousands of products, the chemist was able to work out that these four chemicals only ever really occur together in substances used to kill algae in fish tanks. What's more, only one brand of algae killer called *Algae Destroyer* contained these four chemicals exactly. It appeared that the poisoner may have mixed the medicinal powder and cyanide together

in a bowl that had once been used to crush tablets of *Algae Destroyer*.

Hot on the heels of this discovery came another: Stella Nickell had a fish tank. She had also recently bought some *Algae Destroyer*. (Police had found a pet store owner who remembered selling her the algae killer.) Now the finger of suspicion was pointing Stella's way; and there were more sinister findings to come.

Police discovered that Stella had borrowed some books about human poisoning from the library before her husband's death. At a crime lab, fingerprint experts tested one of these books and found over 80 prints that matched Stella's. Most of these came from the pages of a chapter about cyanide.

Also, Bruce Nickell had a life insurance policy, which said that if he died accidentally, say during a medicine-tampering scare, Stella would get a lot of money. And Stella's daughter had said that her mother had often talked about murdering Bruce.

Now police reckoned they knew what had happened: Stella had put the contaminated bottles of Excedrin in various shops to make it look like her murdered husband had died accidentally during a product-tampering scare. The reason she had alerted the police to Bruce's death was because the doctor who examined Bruce after his death wrongly concluded that he had died naturally of a lung disease. This wasn't what Stella wanted to hear. Under the terms of the life insurance policy, she had to prove that Bruce had died accidentally, say in a product-tampering scare, before she could claim her big pay-out. She needed the police to prove that Bruce had been poisoned accidentally. Instead, they proved that he had been poisoned deliberately.

On 9 May 1988, Stella Nickell was sent to prison for murder.

Types of poison

By the way, if you think poison only comes in the form of a deadly powder or potion, think again! To a toxicologist, a poison is any substance that causes injury or death if it gets into your body. In other words drinking bleach or toilet cleaner counts as poisoning; so too does swallowing a whole bottle of aspirin in one go, or drinking too much alcohol, or breathing in mega amounts of carbon monoxide gas from a car's exhaust pipe, a faulty gas appliance, or a fire.

Past times, past crimes

One of the great things about modern methods of detecting poisons is that they can be used to help solve past crimes. Take the death of Napoleon Bonaparte (1769–1821), for example. For years, many

100

believed that the famous French emperor had died of cancer. But according to a modern pathologist and a modern toxicologist, the great man was poisoned!

Some poisons, such as arsenic, get into the hair, nails or bones of those they kill and stay there long after the victims have been buried. When Napoleon died, his hair was cut from his head by his faithful servants and passed down from one generation to the next as a hairloom – sorry, heirloom. By examining some of this hair, the modern crime-busters have now discovered that the great man died of arsenic poisoning.

A clear-cut case of hair today and gone tomorrow!

MIND OVER MURDER

Crimes are committed for all sorts of reasons. Some dodgy doers commit a crime once and once only. Others carry out similar kinds of crimes over and over again. Those who repeat the same kind of crime are called serial offenders.

YEUCH! THIS CEREAL IS CERTAINLY OFFENSIVE

Catching dangerous serial offenders

The most dangerous kind of serial offender is the serial killer. Detectives out to catch really dangerous serial offenders sometimes ask psychiatrists and psychologists to work out what sort of person they are hunting for. (A psychiatrist is someone trained to understand and treat diseases of the mind. A psychologist is someone trained to study people's minds and behaviour.) Working out what sort of person committed an unsolved crime involves a lot of careful observation and smart guesswork on the part of the psychiatrist or psychologist. They have to study all the clues available; find out about the victims' backgrounds; work out how the criminal probably behaved at each crime scene; and then use these findings to come up with a character description of the criminal. If a psychiatrist suspects that the unknown criminal is suffering from a particular mental illness, he or she can build a character description based on what is known about people who suffer from that particular mental illness.

Once detectives have a character description, or profile, of the unknown criminal, they can check it against the profiles of known criminals and possible suspects.

WE'RE LOOKING FOR A RIGHT VILLAIN HERE, SIR. HE IS A TALL, FAT BLOKE WITH A MOUSTACHE. VERY BOSSY. PROBABLY WEARS A UNIFORM TO WORK ...

The first famous serial offender to be well and truly kippered by a profiler was nicknamed the Mad Bomber – which was a pretty accurate name really, seeing that he was **a)** mad and **b)** a bomber. This is his story:

True Crime Casebook
Case study 9: The Mad Bomber

In 1940 an unexploded bomb was found in New York City in a building belonging to an electricity company called the Consolidated Edison Company, or Con Ed for short. Less than a year later, another unexploded bomb was found near a Con Ed building. With the first bomb came a neatly written note, which read "CON EDISON CROOKS, THIS IS FOR YOU."

A short time later, the USA joined World War II, and the police received a letter from the bomber that said he or she wouldn't be making any more bombs while the war was on, but he or she would in time, "...BRING THE CON EDISON TO JUSTICE – THEY WILL PAY FOR THEIR DASTARDLY DEEDS."

During the war similar letters were received all over New York City. Then the war ended, and more bombs started to appear in the city. This time, some of them went off. Alongside the bombs came more letters – always neatly printed, and always threatening to get even with Con Ed.

The police had no idea who the bomber was or what he or she had against Con Ed. So, in 1956, they took the unusual step of asking psychiatrist Dr James Brussel to come up with a profile of the bomber. These are just some of the things Dr B concluded:

Profile
The bomber has a grudge against Con Ed, possibly because he was sacked or punished by the company.

Reasoning
The content of the letters make the grudge bit obvious.

The bomber is a man.	Throughout history, bombers have nearly always been male.
The bomber is suffering from a serious mental illness called paranoia. 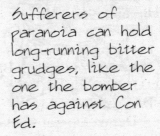	Sufferers of paranoia can hold long-running bitter grudges, like the one the bomber has against Con Ed.
The bomber is middle-aged, i.e. about 40-50 years old. 	Paranoia can take ten years to develop, and usually reaches its peak around age 35. If the bomber was around 30 when the first bomb was planted in 1940, he'd be in his mid-forties in 1956, when his last, and most powerful, bomb went off.

The bomber is neat and tidy.

People with paranoia are often obsessively neat and tidy. (The neatness of the bomber's hand-printed letters and his carefully constructed bombs are a dead giveaway.)

The bomber is educated; his family aren't from the USA.

The letters are fairly well written with no misspellings (sign of an education), but they sound stilted, as though they have been translated into English from another language. Also, the letters contain no slang words or phrases which natural American speakers would use. E.g., New Yorkers say "Con Ed", the bomber says "the Con Ed".

The bomber is a Slav, i.e. his family comes from Eastern or Central Europe, e.g. Poland, the Czech Republic, Serbia, Bulgaria, etc.	Historically, people from Eastern and Central Europe often use bombs when they want to assassinate someone.
The bomber is probably a Roman Catholic.	Most Slavs are Roman Catholic.
The bomber probably lives in the state of Connecticut, which is near New York State, in which is situated New York City.	Some of the bomber's letters have been posted from Westchester County. (The bomber isn't dumb enough to post the letters from his home state.) You have to pass through Westchester County to get from Connecticut to New York City. Many Eastern and Central Europeans live in Connecticut.

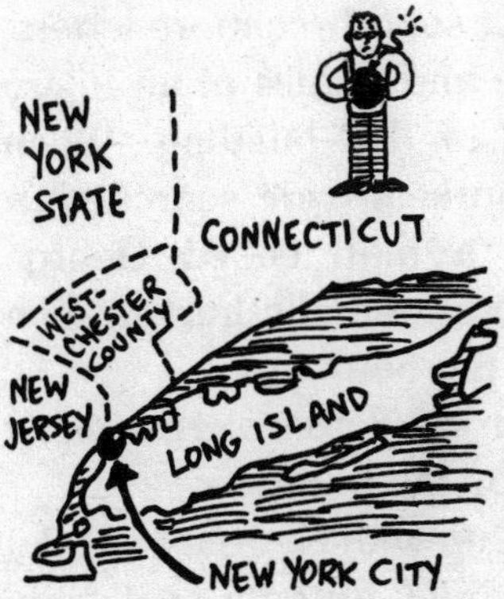

NEW YORK STATE

CONNECTICUT

WEST-CHESTER COUNTY

NEW JERSEY

LONG ISLAND

NEW YORK CITY

When he is arrested, the bomber will be wearing a double-breasted suit - with the buttons done up.

I WANT TO LOOK MY BEST FOR THE PRESS...

The bomber is a neat, tidy, traditional man, and a double-breasted suit is the neatest, most traditional fashion of the 1950s. The buttons will be done up because that's the tidiest way to wear a double-breasted suit jacket.

Once his profile of the bomber was complete, Dr B suggested that it be published in a newspaper. This, the doctor predicted, would prompt the publicity-seeking madman to trip himself up.

And it did.

Immediately the bomber sent three more letters. In one, he gave the date and details of an injury he had suffered in a Con Ed building. When records of ex Con Ed workers were searched, a letter was found from a man called George Metesky who had been accidentally hurt at Con Ed on the date given by the bomber.

Some of the phrases in the letter were exactly the same as those used by the bomber.

When the police caught up with George Metesky in his Connecticut home, they found a neat, tidy, 54-year-old man, suffering from paranoia, whose family had originally come from Poland, and whose garage was stuffed with bomb-making equipment. When the police arrested him, he was wearing a double-breasted suit – buttoned up.

The sixth sense detectives

Spooky though it may seem, there are a few people who appear to have extraordinary unexplained powers the rest off us lack (and no, I'm not talking about your ability to burp to order!). On occasions, these incredible powers have been used to help crack crime. Take this mind-bending murder mystery, for example:

The "detective" who could read minds

On 9 July 1928, in Alberta, Canada, a farmer called Vernon Booher came home to find his mum and brother lying dead on the floor of their farmhouse. In nearby outbuildings lay the bodies of two farm workers. All four bodies had been shot with a .303 rifle, which was nowhere to be found.

109

Stumped for a solution to the case, the chief of police called in Dr Maximilien Langsner, who was said to be able to "read" the minds of other people.

Dr Langsner listened carefully to everything the Canadian police had to say about the murder case. Then he dropped a bombshell.

"The killer is Vernon Booher, and the murder weapon is hidden at the back of the farmhouse."

"Are you sure?" asked the chief of police, saucer-eyed.

"Absolutely," replied the doctor: and to prove his point, he led police to a clump of grass behind the farmhouse in which lay hidden the murder weapon.

"But what proof do you have that Vernon is the killer?" asked the police chief. "The gun has been wiped clean of fingerprints."

"I've no proof," replied Dr Langsner, calmly. "But if you put Vernon in a cell and let me sit outside it, I'll tell you how he committed the crime."

The chief of police agreed to this request, and Dr Langsner positioned himself outside Vernon's cell. For much of the time he was there, neither he nor Vernon spoke a word.

"So, what did you learn?" asked the chief of police when he met up with Dr Langsner again.

I BET YOU'VE NEVER HEARD OF "GOOD COP, BAD COP, PSYCHIC COP", EH, VERNON?

"Vernon stole the murder weapon from a neighbour, and shot his mother. Believing his brother and the two farm workers had witnessed the crime, he shot them, too."

110

It was true that a .303 rifle had been stolen from one of Vernon's neighbours whilst the neighbour had been at church the previous Sunday. But Vernon had also been at church that day, so how could he have stolen the murder weapon?

"Find the small woman with a long jaw and tiny eyes who sat at the back of the church last Sunday," said Dr Langsner. "She saw Vernon sneak out to steal the rifle."

WHY THE LONG FACE?

The police found the woman Dr Langsner had described, and she confirmed that Vernon had indeed snuck out of church the previous Sunday. In front of witnesses, she told Vernon what she'd seen and he, realizing the game was up, confessed to the killings.

Strange but true

If you think Dr Langsner's unexplained powers are a one-off, check out these other true tales:

In 1956 a young woman went missing in South Africa. The police were having no luck solving her disappearance, so her family turned to a retired headmaster who had an amazing ability. Simply by holding an object, the ex-headmaster could locate the person who owned it.

The ex-headmaster was given some clothing belonging to the missing woman; and in a darkened room, he placed his hands on the clothes, closed his eyes, and remained silent for a few minutes. Then he spoke. The young woman was dead, he said, and her body was lying in water several miles from her home.

A group of searchers, led by the ex-headmaster, went to the spot he had described and there, sure enough, they found the missing woman's lifeless body. It turned out she'd been shot by a man she knew who lived near her home.

In 1827 a young woman was murdered by her boyfriend and buried under the floor of a red barn in Suffolk, England. Soon after the murder, the victim's stepmother began to have nightmares about a red barn whose floor opened up to reveal her stepdaughter's corpse. The dream even revealed the exact spot under which the body had been buried. Suspecting the dream to be a message sent by his dead daughter, her father located the red barn, sneaked inside, and, in the exact spot his wife had described, he found the buried body of his daughter.

In 1979 a young Russian girl failed to return home after going skating. A photo of the girl, together with some of her schoolwork was sent to a woman in Britain who was known for her psychic powers. The minute the woman received the photo and schoolwork, she "saw" what had happened: the poor girl had been strangled to death by a big, brown-haired man, aged about 30, with a round face and a beard.

This information was sent to the Russian police, who already had a suspect that fitted this description. When the suspect was questioned more thoroughly, he broke down and confessed to the murder.

TRUTH, LIES AND TINY SPIES

Suppose someone has stolen a stash of cash from your family's safe. You think you know the identity of the sneaky safecracker, but you have no evidence to prove your suspicions. How do you get your suspect to confess to the crime? Do you use...

a) bribes   **b)** threats   **c)** torture?

The police aren't allowed to force suspects into making confessions. But they can interview them to try to find the truth. During an interview a suspect is given the chance to explain his or her side of the story, and the police ask questions about any bits of that story that don't add up. The idea is to let someone who is fibbing trap themselves in their own web of lies.

Of course, this plan doesn't always work, so the police sometimes have to try other means to get the proof they need. Some crime investigators believe that a good way to get to the truth is to wire up a suspect to a lie-detecting machine called a polygraph. A polygraph picks up changes to a person's breathing, heartbeat, sweating and blood pressure during questioning. The operator of the machine starts by asking questions about all kinds of everyday things, and then moves on to asking questions about the crime. The idea is that a guilty person's breathing, heartbeat and pulse, will react more strongly to these questions than to the ordinary questions.

HOWEVER, before you wire your mum up to a polygraph to see whether she really has been snooping about in your bedroom, take note. Not all criminal investigators are convinced that the polygraph is a good thing. Some reckon that the results it gives aren't always accurate, and that it is possible to beat the machine.

DIY detection: the trap

You suspect someone is entering your bedroom on the sly, so you decide to test your suspicion using some of the stuff in your pockets. How?

Answer: You cut a few centimetres of the invisible thread and tape one end of it to the bottom of your bedroom door. Then you pull the door almost closed, and stick the other end of the tape to the doorframe. If, on your return, you find the thread has moved, you know someone has been in your bedroom.

Under surveillance

Another method crime investigators use to try to get to the truth is covert surveillance (that's spying to you and me). This kind of undercover work is generally divided into three areas: mobile surveillance, static surveillance and technical surveillance.

Mobile surveillance involves a surveillance operator, or operators, following a suspect by car, motorbike, boat, or on foot.

FEMALE SURVEILLANCE OPERATOR CARRYING A HIDDEN RADIO SYSTEM

117

Static surveillance involves a surveillance operator, or operators, keeping a close watch on a suspect, criminal, or place where it's believed a crime might be committed from a stationary position, such as from the inside of a surveillance van.

FILM ON REAR WINDOWS LETS SURVEILLANCE OPERATORS SEE OUT WITHOUT ANYONE BEING ABLE TO SEE IN

IMAGE INTENSIFIER FITTED TO A VIDEO CAMERA ALLOWS OPERATOR TO VIDEO IN DARKNESS. THE INTENSIFIER MAGNIFIES LIGHT IN THE SKY THAT WE CAN'T SEE, FROM STARS, THE MOON ETC, BY A MILLION TIMES

CAMERA

COMPUTER

Crime-cracking fact

For years, law enforcers in the USA have trapped deer poachers using static surveillance and a remote-controlled model of a deer. The model is placed in a suitable spot, and an operator using a remote control up to a quarter of a mile away, moves the animal's head and tail to make it appear alive. As soon as a poacher takes aim at the bionic Bambi, police hiding nearby video tape the crime, and move in to arrest the poacher.

INTERIOR PANELLED WITH PLYWOOD AND PAINTED BLACK HELPS PROTECT OPERATORS FROM THE COLD AND MAKES THE VAN MORE SOUNDPROOF

ALARM, OPERATED BY SWITCH FROM INSIDE, KEEPS NOSEY PEOPLE AWAY

MAGNETIC SIGN CAN BE REMOVED TO CHANGE VAN'S APPEARANCE

SURVEILLANCE VAN

Technical surveillance involves a surveillance operator, or operators, gathering information using technical equipment such as bugs (electronic eavesdropping devices), tape recorders, video recorders, and vehicle-tracking equipment.

MICROPHONE

TRANSMITTER

A MICROPHONE HIDDEN INSIDE THE PLUG SOCKET PICKS UP THE CONVERSATION; A RADIO TRANSMITTER ATTACHED TO THE MICROPHONE TRANSMITS THE SIGNAL OVER THE AIR TO A RECEIVER IN THE LOFT, WHICH IS CONNECTED TO HEADPHONES

A TINY VIDEO CAMERA HIDDEN IN THE ALARM SYSTEM STARTS RECORDING WHENEVER MOVEMENT IS DETECTED

MICROPHONE

TRANSMITTER

SWITCH

BATTERY

A TINY RADIO BUG TRANSMITS BOTH SIDES OF A PHONE CONVERSATION TO A RECEIVING UNIT IN THE CELLAR WHICH IS CONNECTED TO A TAPE RECORDER. A SWITCH ACTIVATES THE BUG EVERY TIME THE HANDSET IS PICKED UP

Follow that car!

One way of keeping track of a suspect vehicle is to secretly fit it with a Global Positioning System (GPS) receiver. Navigation satellites high above the Earth send signals that are picked up by the GPS receiver. From these signals the GPS receiver calculates the vehicle's position to within a few metres. This information is then sent over a phone or radio network to a receiving computer, which displays the car's position on an electronic map.

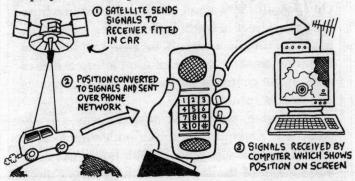

① SATELLITE SENDS SIGNALS TO RECEIVER FITTED IN CAR

② POSITION CONVERTED TO SIGNALS AND SENT OVER PHONE NETWORK

③ SIGNALS RECEIVED BY COMPUTER WHICH SHOWS POSITION ON SCREEN

Law enforcers in the USA have trapped a number of car thieves using a "bait" car, fitted with a hidden video camera and a tracking device. The "bait" car is left unlocked, with its keys in the ignition, in an area known for car thefts. As soon as a thief tries to drive the car, its doors automatically lock, and an operator using a remote control turns off its engine. Police following in a surveillance vehicle then move in to arrest the carjacker, confident that the crime has been captured by the tiny video camera. Should something happen and the car's engine fails to cut out, the getaway can be tracked using the hidden tracking device.

CCTV to the rescue

Nowadays many public places, such as shopping centres, banks, and streets, are watched over by video cameras called closed-circuit television, or CCTV for short. These cameras have helped catch all sorts of villains including the London nail bomber.

True Crime Casebook
Case study 10: The London Nail Bomber

On 17 April 1999 a nail bomb exploded in a busy shopping street in south London. One week later, a similar bomb went off in east London. The following week, a third explosion let rip a hail of nails in the centre of the capital. Horrific injuries and deaths resulted.

A massive police investigation was quickly launched. Over 1,000 CCTV videotapes were checked. (That's around 26,000 hours worth of film.) Many of the tapes held images from more than one CCTV camera, which meant that each frame on a tape often contained several pictures, each from a different camera.

Fortunately, eyewitnesses had spotted the sports bag in which the first bomb had been left. So police scanned the south London CCTV coverage for people carrying the same type of bag as that left at the bombsite. Eventually, they struck lucky and found two tiny images: the first showed someone carrying the same type of bag as the bomber's; the second showed the same person without the bag. However, because these images were so small and blurred, it was

---

impossible to tell what the suspect looked like. So, they had to be sent to experts in the UK and abroad to be enlarged.

In the meantime, more pictures of a man with, and then without, a suspicious-looking sports bag, were found on other CCTV videotapes. When these pictures were printed in newspapers, someone recognized the suspect and identified him to police as David Copeland.

Police quickly traced David Copeland to his home, and he immediately confessed to planting the bombs. His motive for the crimes had been hatred: hatred of the sorts of people who lived or hung out in the areas bombed.

On 30 June 2000 David Copeland was sentenced to life in prison.

EPILOGUE

AND NOW... "THAT'S CRIMINAL!" — THE TV CRIME PROGRAMME THAT HELPS YOU SLEEP EASIER AT NIGHT

CRIMETIME TV

AS READERS OF THIS CLUED-UP BOOK WILL KNOW...

That's CRIMINAL

The Knowledge

crafty CRIME-busTING

CRIME-BUSTERS DO NOT ONLY RELY ON SLEUTHING SKILLS TO COLLAR CRIMINALS.

THEY ALSO USE TECHNOLOGY AND SCIENCE, AS THESE HEADLINES REMIND US

THE CRIMINAL ENQUIRER

WORLD'S FIRST NATIONAL DNA DATABASE MAKES 900 DNA PROFILE MATCHES A WEEK

CRIME TIMES

UK'S LEADING FORENSIC SCIENCE ORGANIZATION DEALS WITH 100,000 CASES A YEAR

DNA TODAY

SCIENTISTS PRODUCE DNA PROFILE FROM SPECK OF DANDRUFF

CASE CLOSED

126